Jim in Training

Ben Butterworth and Bill Stockdale
Illustrated by Maureen and Gordon Gray

Methuen

Titles in the series

First published 1975 by Methuen Educational Ltd
11 New Fetter Lane, London EC4P 4EE
Text © 1975 Ben Butterworth and Bill Stockdale
Illustrations © 1975 Methuen Educational Ltd
Filmset in Photon Times 18 on 26 pt by
Richard Clay (The Chaucer Press), Ltd, Bungay, Suffolk
and printed in Great Britain by
Fletcher & Son Ltd, Norwich

ISBN 0 423 89370 X

Jim in Training

'Well, Jim,' said Colonel Johnson,
'you have been working with me
for a long time now, and I think
you are ready for promotion.
I am going to send you
to our agents' training camp
where you will learn
all the latest tricks.
The camp will tell me how you get on.'

1

'I have sent a girl to train with you.

She is a new agent called Olga

and she is at the camp now.

You should get on well together,

but take care

as that camp can be a rough place,

and you never know

where Bratt's men will turn up next.

Now, get down there
as soon as you can,
and take your dog Radar with you.'

The camp was on an old airfield.

Jim stopped his Jensen at the gates
and looked round.

'Goodness, Radar,' he said,
'this place is miles from anywhere.

Let's hope that Olga will liven it up.

Come on, boy, we had better go in.'

A very tall man came up to them.

'Jim Hunter?' he asked.

'That's me,' said Jim.

'I'm John Watkins, your instructor,'
said the tall man,

'but everyone calls me Little John.
This is Ken, my assistant.'

Ken smiled and picked up Jim's case.

'Come on,' he said,

'I'll show you to your room.'

As Jim was unpacking,
there was a tap at the door
and a pretty, dark haired girl
came into the room.
'Hello, you must be Olga,' said Jim,
and held out his hand.

A second later he was flat on his back.

'I'm a Black Belt,' said the girl.

'You should have made sure first

that I was Olga.

This is a training school, you know.

I'll see you tomorrow.'

9

The next day
Little John was waiting for him.
'Right, Jim Hunter,' he said,
'here's an easy job to begin with.
I want you to put a limpet mine
on the old boat
at the bottom of the lake.'

Jim looked at Olga.
'Come on,' he said,
'let's take the plunge.'
They swam slowly
to the middle of the lake.

Jim had dived deep down to the boat,
when he began to feel sleepy.
He knew he must be very short of air,
so, leaving the mine,
he kicked hard for the surface.

Olga was waiting for him at the top.

'I reckon somebody

has fixed this gear,' said Jim,

when he had got his breath back.

'Those air bottles

should last for ages.

That's very odd indeed.'

'I'm sorry about your diving gear,'
said Little John the next morning,
'but always check the bottles yourself
before you go under the water.
I hope you have more luck in the air.

Olga will show you
how to work this jet pack.
I know you like birds, and now
you can learn to fly like one!'
'I like the sort without wings best,'
laughed Jim. 'Girls!'

'Keep above the lake, just in case,'
said Ken, as Jim got ready
to fire the jets.
'OK,' said Jim, 'here we go.'

He pulled the control lever
and shot up into the air.
'Take care,' shouted Olga.

Suddenly the left jet cut out
and Jim began to spin like a top
before crashing down into the water.

'That was bad luck,' said Ken
as he helped Jim out of the lake.
'You must have had a dud jet.'
'I am beginning to think that someone
wants me out of the way,' said Jim.
'I wonder what will happen next.'

'We will do a bit
of indoor work today,'
Little John told Jim
when they met the next morning.
'We'd better find out
how much noise you can stand.'
'My yoga is still pretty good,'
said Jim, 'let's give it a try.'

Little John switched on the tape
and turned up the loudspeakers.
The noise crashed into the room,
and Jim and Olga went into a trance.
'Well done,' said Little John.
'You would not have any trouble there.
Now, let's look at a new device.'

'This is our very latest lie detector. It's very small and it can be used on a person without his knowing.'
'Good. Beam it on Olga,' said Jim. 'There is something I'd like to ask her.'

'Tell me, Olga,' said Jim,
'that empty air bottle and dud jet
were fixed on purpose weren't they?'
'Of course not,' Olga replied.
'Who would want to do
something like that?'
'That's what I would like to know,'
said Jim.

He went back to Little John,

who was grinning.

'I don't know what you asked her,'

he said, 'but she was lying to you.

The needle went right over!'

'Now,' said Little John,

'sit down and try one of these.'

He gave Jim a long cigarette.

'A good puff of smoke in Olga's face,

will put her in a daze

for about ten seconds.'

'Here goes,' said Jim.

He blew a cloud of smoke at the girl,

then emptied her handbag

on to the table.

When Olga came round again,

she looked at her bag in surprise.

'How on earth did you manage that?'

she asked. 'I never saw a thing.'

'Just another of my tricks,' said Jim.

29

'This is a much stronger cigarette,'
said Little John, handing one to Jim.
'In fact it is a killer.
It fires poison darts
five seconds after it is lit.
If a dart hits you,
you die in a second.
I'll light one and show you
how to hit a target.'

Little John lit the cigarette,

but instead of going forward,

the dart hissed back into his face,

and he fell on the floor in a heap.

Jim and Olga bent over him.

'He's dead,' Olga whispered.

'Someone in this camp is a killer,'
said Jim, 'and that dart
wasn't meant for Little John,
it was meant for me.'

'Quick, I need your help, Olga.
I'm going to use the lie detector
on every person in this camp.'

While Jim asked questions
Olga watched the needle,
but it never moved.
No one knew anything
about the cigarette.

Jim handed the lie detector

back to Ken.

'You look after this, Ken,' he said.

'I had better take Olga

for something to eat.

She looks a bit shaken up.'

'I'm sorry about Little John,'

said Olga,

when they had finished eating.

'I wish we knew who killed him.'

'I intend to find out,' said Jim,

'before someone else gets killed.'

'My father was killed three years ago,'

said Olga, 'so I became an agent

to help me find his killer.'

'I was wondering why
you started in this racket,' said Jim.
'Tell me more while we have coffee.'
'I'm afraid I must be off,' said Olga,
looking at her watch.
'A message came that I have been
ordered back to London.
I expect we'll meet again there.'

As Olga left the room, Ken came in
and went quickly over to Jim.

'Were you trying to date her?'

he asked.

'No,' Jim replied.

'I'm not in the mood

for dating girls just now.'

'Well, I had the lie detector on her,'
Ken went on.

'She was telling you a pack of lies.'

'Of course!' Jim shouted.

'She's the one! Look out,
she may have left us a present.

I bet it's a bomb.

Here, Radar, find it, boy.'

Radar jumped up from Jim's feet
and sniffed about the room.
He stood still, with his nose
pointing to the table mat.

'A heat bomb!' gasped Jim.

'If I had put a hot cup of coffee

on that mat,

it would have been the end of me.

No wonder Olga

was in such a hurry to go.'

Jim rushed out of the room
and ran to the car park,
but Olga's red Spitfire had gone.
Was she bluffing, or had she
really gone to London?

Jim jumped into his car

and shot out on to the road.

He would have to catch up with her

before she turned

on to the motorway to London.

There was no traffic on this road,
and Jim's Jensen got up to ninety
in a few seconds.
He had been given driving lessons
on the race track,
but he would need all his skill
to catch Olga's red Spitfire
on this winding road
without causing an accident.

Five minutes later,
in the beam of his headlights,
Jim spotted the Spitfire in front.
He gripped the wheel
and put his foot hard down.
Gradually, the Jensen came level
with Olga's car.

Jim saw Olga look across at him.

She looked pale and frightened.

Jim moved the Jensen

nearer and nearer

to the side of the red car.

'Now, Radar,' he said,
'we will find out who has
the strongest nerves.
Someone has to give way,
and it won't be me!'

Jim felt a bump
as the two cars touched.
Olga's face was white, and
she seemed to be shouting something.

Jim pulled his car away,
then he went in towards her again,
but a little harder than before.
The Spitfire was forced slowly
to the side of the road
but Olga still kept going.
Jim gritted his teeth.
'Right, Radar,' he said,
'she's in for it this time.
Hold on, boy.'

Jim pushed his Jensen
against the Spitfire
for the last time.

They were on a bend,
and Olga's nerve gave way.
She braked hard
and swung the wheel round.
With a screech of brakes
her car skidded
and turned over on the grass bank.
Olga was flung out
and landed on her back
a few yards from the car.

Jim pulled up in a flash and ran back.

He picked Olga up

and put her in his car.

'You little fool,' he said,

'you could have been killed.

We will see what

Colonel Johnson says

when he hears about this.'

The Colonel looked up
as Jim went into his office
with Olga holding on to his arm.
She was still white and shaken.
'One of Bratt's ladies, I think,'
said Jim, nodding at Olga.
'No, Jim, she is one of ours,
in spite of all that she has done,'
the Colonel replied with a smile.
'You see, Jim, this was a put-up job.
I wanted to see if you
were ready for promotion.
Olga was trained to test you.'

'So it was all a put-up job, was it?'
said Jim, looking angry.
'Dud diving gear, dud jet pack,
dud poison dart
and dud heat bomb too, I suppose.
I've really been taken for a ride.'
'Not a bit, Jim,' said the Colonel.
'Little John has just rung up
to say how impressed he is with
the speed that you found his "killer".'

Then the Colonel turned to Olga.

'How do you think he made out?'

he asked with a smile.

'Almost too well,' Olga replied.

'He very nearly killed me

with that car of his.

I don't want to test him again, thanks.

He's too much for me.'